PRINCEWILL LAGANG

Sailing to Success: Larry Ellison's Life Lessons from America's Cup to Oracle's Helm

First published by PRINCEWILL LAGANG 2023

Copyright © 2023 by Princewill Lagang

All rights reserved. No part of this publication may be reproduced, stored or transmitted in any form or by any means, electronic, mechanical, photocopying, recording, scanning, or otherwise without written permission from the publisher. It is illegal to copy this book, post it to a website, or distribute it by any other means without permission.

Princewill Lagang asserts the moral right to be identified as the author of this work.

First edition

*This book was professionally typeset on Reedsy.
Find out more at reedsy.com*

Contents

1	Setting Sail	1
2	Charting Uncharted Waters	4
3	Sailing the Digital Seas: Oracle's Evolution in the 21st...	7
4	Beyond Business: Larry Ellison's Impact Beyond the Boardroom	10
5	Mastering the Waves of Change: Larry Ellison's Leadership...	13
6	Legacy Unveiled: Larry Ellison's Enduring Impact	16
7	Sailing Forward: Oracle's Continuing Odyssey in a Dynamic...	19
8	Beyond Boundaries: Oracle's Impact on the Digital Frontier	22
9	A Tapestry of Success: Larry Ellison's Enduring Legacy	25
10	Sailing Into Tomorrow: Oracle's Future Horizons	28
11	Reflections and Resonance: Larry Ellison's Lasting Impact	32
12	The Unfinished Symphony: Oracle's Future Symphony	35
13	Summary	38

1

Setting Sail

Title: Sailing to Success: Larry Ellison's Life Lessons from America's Cup to Oracle's Helm

The sun dipped below the horizon, casting a warm glow over the Pacific Ocean as Larry Ellison stood on the deck of his luxurious yacht, Oracle Team USA, slicing through the waves. The rhythmic sound of the water against the hull echoed the journey of a man whose life mirrored the ebb and flow of the vast sea. This is where the story begins—the story of a man who not only conquered the maritime challenges of the America's Cup but also navigated the complex waters of the technology industry.

The Genesis of Ambition

Larry Ellison's journey didn't start on the ocean. It began in the heart of Chicago, where he was born to a single mother in 1944. Raised by his aunt and uncle, Ellison's early life was marked by adversity. However, adversity often breeds resilience, and young Larry was no exception. His inquisitive mind and natural knack for problem-solving laid the groundwork for a brilliant future that would unfold in unexpected ways.

The seed of ambition took root during his college years at the University of Chicago, where Ellison discovered his passion for computer science. The nascent world of technology beckoned, and he eagerly embraced the opportunities it presented. Dropping out of college proved to be a strategic move as he immersed himself in the burgeoning Silicon Valley of the 1970s.

Navigating the Silicon Seas

As the tech industry burgeoned, so did Ellison's ambitions. In 1977, he co-founded a company that would eventually be named Oracle Corporation. From the outset, Ellison demonstrated a remarkable ability to anticipate the industry's needs and chart a course for success. Oracle became a pioneering force in the world of relational databases, forever altering the landscape of information management.

Ellison's leadership style emerged as a unique blend of vision, audacity, and an unyielding commitment to innovation. The metaphorical seas of the technology industry presented challenges, but Ellison, with an unwavering determination, sailed through them. Oracle's growth mirrored his own ascent to prominence, and by the 1990s, it had become a global giant, a testament to Ellison's leadership at the helm.

Hoisting the Sails of America's Cup

Yet, success for Ellison was not confined to the digital realm. His passion for sailing became a parallel journey—one that would mirror his approach to business. In 2010, Ellison achieved a lifelong dream by winning the America's Cup, the oldest trophy in international sport. The victory was not just a testament to his sailing prowess but a reflection of his philosophy: no challenge is too great, and no goal too ambitious.

The America's Cup victory was more than a trophy; it was a symbol of Ellison's ability to leverage technology, strategy, and human ingenuity to overcome obstacles. It showcased a man who embraced risk, embraced challenges, and emerged victorious against all odds.

Embarking on the Journey Ahead

As we set sail into the deeper waters of Larry Ellison's life, we will navigate through the highs and lows, the triumphs and setbacks that shaped the man behind the iconic persona. This journey is not just a biography; it is a manual for success, a chronicle of life lessons drawn from the synergy of sailing and Silicon Valley.

Join us as we explore the chapters of a life well-lived, a life defined by the relentless pursuit of excellence—whether racing on the open sea or steering one of the world's most influential technology companies. Larry Ellison's story is a beacon for those who dare to dream and aspire to sail to success against the winds of adversity.

2

Charting Uncharted Waters

Title: Navigating Innovation: Oracle's Rise to Prominence

As Larry Ellison hoisted the sails of success with Oracle Corporation, the company's journey was akin to a bold expedition into uncharted waters. Chapter 2 dives into the heart of Ellison's leadership and Oracle's rise, exploring the innovation, challenges, and strategic decisions that shaped both the man and the company.

The Silicon Valley Odyssey

The late 20th century marked the golden era of Silicon Valley, and Oracle, under Ellison's visionary guidance, emerged as a key player. Chapter 2 delves into the company's early days, from its foundation in 1977 to the release of the groundbreaking Oracle Database in 1979. Ellison's unorthodox approach to business, his willingness to take risks, and his emphasis on product excellence set Oracle on a trajectory that would define the software industry.

The Database Revolution

At the heart of Oracle's success was its pioneering work in relational databases. Ellison's vision for a robust, scalable, and efficient database system fueled the company's growth. The relational database not only became a technological cornerstone for businesses but also established Oracle as a leader in the industry. Chapter 2 explores the technical innovations that propelled Oracle to the forefront and Ellison's role in steering the ship through the turbulent seas of competition.

Strategic Acquisitions and Global Expansion

Ellison's strategic acumen extended beyond product development. Recognizing the importance of diversification and expansion, Oracle embarked on a series of strategic acquisitions. Chapter 2 unveils the stories behind key acquisitions like Sun Microsystems, PeopleSoft, and Siebel Systems, illustrating how Ellison strategically broadened Oracle's portfolio, transforming it into a comprehensive provider of enterprise solutions.

Simultaneously, Oracle expanded its global footprint, becoming a multinational powerhouse. Ellison's leadership style, marked by a blend of ambition and calculated risk-taking, played a pivotal role in Oracle's ability to navigate diverse markets and cultural landscapes.

The Dot-Com Boom and Bust

The late 1990s brought both unprecedented growth and challenges to the tech industry, culminating in the dot-com boom. Chapter 2 scrutinizes Oracle's role in this transformative period, exploring how Ellison navigated the company through the boom, maintained financial stability, and adapted to the subsequent burst of the dot-com bubble. The lessons learned during this tumultuous time would shape Oracle's resilience and preparedness for future disruptions.

A Leader's Legacy

As Oracle continued to flourish, Ellison's leadership style left an indelible mark on the company's culture. Chapter 2 concludes with an exploration of the leadership principles that defined Oracle under Ellison's guidance. From fostering a culture of innovation to prioritizing customer satisfaction, Ellison's leadership legacy permeated every facet of the organization.

Join us as we unravel the intricacies of Oracle's ascent to prominence, a journey guided by Larry Ellison's unique vision, technological foresight, and a relentless pursuit of excellence. Chapter 2 is a chronicle of innovation, determination, and strategic prowess that laid the foundation for the chapters that follow in this tale of success on both the high seas and the digital frontier.

3

Sailing the Digital Seas: Oracle's Evolution in the 21st Century

Title: Beyond Databases: Clouds, Challenges, and Larry Ellison's Vision

As the 21st century dawned, Larry Ellison found himself at the helm of Oracle, navigating the company through a rapidly changing technological landscape. Chapter 3 explores the challenges and triumphs of Oracle's evolution in an era dominated by the emergence of cloud computing, artificial intelligence, and a new wave of digital transformation.

Embracing the Cloud Revolution

The early 2000s witnessed a paradigm shift in the tech industry with the advent of cloud computing. Chapter 3 unfolds the story of how Larry Ellison, known for his visionary approach, recognized the transformative potential of cloud technology. Oracle pivoted to embrace the cloud, marking a departure from its traditional on-premises software model. Ellison's commitment to innovation and adaptability enabled Oracle to position itself as a key player in the cloud computing space.

The Acquisition Game Continues

To fortify its position in the cloud arena, Oracle engaged in a series of strategic acquisitions. Chapter 3 sheds light on key acquisitions such as NetSuite and Taleo, exploring how these moves complemented Oracle's cloud strategy and expanded its capabilities. Ellison's strategic mindset and ability to integrate new technologies into the Oracle ecosystem played a crucial role in the company's sustained relevance.

Navigating Security Concerns

The digital seas brought not only opportunities but also challenges, and chief among them was the increasing importance of cybersecurity. Chapter 3 delves into how Ellison, ever the tactician, led Oracle in addressing the growing concerns surrounding data security. The company invested heavily in developing robust security solutions, acknowledging that in the interconnected digital world, safeguarding data was paramount.

The Autonomous Database and AI Innovation

Ellison's fascination with artificial intelligence became a driving force in Oracle's evolution. Chapter 3 explores the development of the Autonomous Database, a groundbreaking technology that exemplified Oracle's commitment to innovation. By leveraging machine learning and automation, Oracle aimed to revolutionize database management, reducing complexity and enhancing performance. Ellison's foresight in embracing AI technologies positioned Oracle as a frontrunner in the era of intelligent databases.

Corporate Social Responsibility and Environmental Stewardship

As Oracle expanded its influence globally, Ellison recognized the importance of corporate social responsibility and environmental stewardship. Chapter 3 uncovers Oracle's initiatives in sustainability, diversity, and community engagement under Ellison's leadership. The company's commitment to making a positive impact beyond the realm of technology reflects Ellison's broader vision for responsible corporate citizenship.

Lessons from the Digital Voyage

Chapter 3 not only narrates the technological advancements and business strategies that defined Oracle's trajectory in the 21st century but also extracts valuable lessons from Ellison's approach to leadership during this transformative period. From embracing change to fostering innovation and addressing societal responsibilities, Ellison's leadership philosophy provides a compass for navigating the ever-evolving digital seas.

Join us as we navigate through the waves of change, innovation, and challenges that shaped Oracle's journey in the 21st century. Chapter 3 is a testament to Larry Ellison's continued prowess as a strategic navigator, steering Oracle through the complex currents of the digital age.

4

Beyond Business: Larry Ellison's Impact Beyond the Boardroom

Title: A Philanthropic Voyage: Investing in Humanity

As Larry Ellison continued to steer Oracle through the dynamic waters of the tech industry, another facet of his life became increasingly prominent — his dedication to philanthropy. Chapter 4 delves into Ellison's journey beyond business, exploring the philanthropic endeavors that have marked his commitment to making a positive impact on the world.

The Ellison Medical Foundation

In the early 2000s, Ellison turned his attention to the field of medical research. Chapter 4 unravels the story of the Ellison Medical Foundation, an organization dedicated to supporting breakthroughs in understanding aging and age-related diseases. Ellison's personal investment in scientific research showcased his belief in the power of technology to extend beyond business solutions and contribute to advancements in healthcare.

Educational Initiatives and The Lawrence Ellison Institute for Transformative Medicine

Education became another focal point of Ellison's philanthropic efforts. Chapter 4 sheds light on his contributions to educational initiatives, including support for charter schools and higher education. Ellison's vision extended to the establishment of The Lawrence Ellison Institute for Transformative Medicine at the University of Southern California, emphasizing the intersection of technology and medicine to revolutionize healthcare.

America's Cup and Youth Sailing

Ellison's love for sailing extended beyond personal pursuits to initiatives that nurtured young talent. Chapter 4 explores how his involvement in the America's Cup went beyond competition, with a commitment to promoting youth sailing programs. Ellison's philanthropy in this domain aimed to inspire the next generation of sailors, combining his passion for the sport with a desire to create opportunities for aspiring young mariners.

Environmental Conservation and The Lanai Community

As a steward of the environment, Ellison's philanthropy extended to conservation efforts. Chapter 4 uncovers his commitment to sustainable practices on the island of Lanai, which he purchased in 2012. From renewable energy projects to ecological preservation, Ellison's initiatives reflect a broader commitment to environmental sustainability and responsible land management.

Disaster Relief and Global Impact

In times of crisis, Ellison's philanthropy extended to disaster relief efforts. Chapter 4 explores instances where Oracle's founder provided financial support and resources in response to natural disasters, showcasing a commitment to leveraging his influence for the greater good on a global scale.

A Philanthropic Legacy

Chapter 4 not only narrates Ellison's philanthropic initiatives but also reflects on the broader impact of his charitable work. From advancing scientific research to promoting education, youth development, environmental sustainability, and global welfare, Ellison's philanthropy serves as a testament to the idea that success in business can be a powerful force for positive change in the world.

Join us as we explore the philanthropic endeavors that define Larry Ellison's legacy beyond the boardroom. Chapter 4 is a voyage into the heart of compassion and social responsibility, demonstrating how a titan of technology can also be a catalyst for positive transformation in the broader human experience.

5

Mastering the Waves of Change: Larry Ellison's Leadership Philosophy

Title: The Captain's Code: Leadership Lessons from Larry Ellison

As Larry Ellison's journey through the seas of business, technology, and philanthropy continued, a profound aspect of his legacy emerged — his distinctive leadership philosophy. Chapter 5 delves into the core principles and values that have shaped Ellison's approach to leadership, unraveling the captain's code that guided him through the storms and calms of a storied career.

Visionary Leadership: Navigating the Horizon

At the heart of Ellison's leadership philosophy is an unwavering commitment to visionary thinking. Chapter 5 explores how Ellison's ability to anticipate technological trends and envision the future has been a driving force behind Oracle's success. His knack for identifying opportunities on the horizon, whether in databases, cloud computing, or artificial intelligence, set the course for Oracle's evolution.

Embracing Risk: Sailing into the Unknown

Ellison's leadership is characterized by a bold willingness to embrace risk. Chapter 5 uncovers the calculated gambles he took throughout his career, from pioneering relational databases to steering Oracle into the cloud. Ellison's fearlessness in the face of uncertainty serves as a lesson in the art of calculated risk-taking, a quality that has propelled both him and Oracle to new heights.

Innovation as a Constant Wind

Innovation is the lifeblood of Ellison's leadership. Chapter 5 explores how he cultivated a culture of constant innovation at Oracle, emphasizing the need to adapt and evolve in the ever-changing tech landscape. Whether through groundbreaking products like the Autonomous Database or strategic acquisitions, Ellison's commitment to pushing the boundaries of what is possible has been a driving force behind Oracle's enduring relevance.

Customer-Centric Approach: Sailing with the Crew

Ellison understands the importance of keeping the customer at the center of the journey. Chapter 5 delves into how a customer-centric approach has been a guiding principle for Oracle under Ellison's leadership. From tailoring solutions to addressing customer needs, this philosophy has not only ensured customer satisfaction but has also built enduring relationships that withstand the test of time.

Adaptability in the Face of Storms

In the turbulent waters of the tech industry, adaptability is paramount. Chapter 5 explores how Ellison's leadership philosophy encourages adaptability, emphasizing the need to pivot and transform when faced with challenges. From the dot-com bubble burst to the rise of the cloud, Ellison's ability to navigate storms and emerge stronger exemplifies the resilience embedded in his leadership style.

Mentorship and Building Strong Crews

Ellison's leadership isn't just about navigating solo; it's about building a strong crew. Chapter 5 examines his commitment to mentorship and fostering a collaborative work environment. Ellison's recognition of the importance of a talented and motivated team reflects a leadership philosophy that extends beyond individual success to the collective achievements of the entire organization.

Legacy and the Enduring Wake

As we reflect on Ellison's leadership philosophy, Chapter 5 concludes by examining the enduring wake he leaves behind. From pioneering technologies to philanthropic endeavors and a distinct approach to leadership, Ellison's legacy is one of vision, resilience, and a commitment to leaving the world a better place.

Join us as we explore the leadership principles that have guided Larry Ellison's illustrious career. Chapter 5 is a captain's log of wisdom, offering valuable insights and lessons from a leader who has weathered the storms and sailed to success against the backdrop of a rapidly evolving sea of change.

6

Legacy Unveiled: Larry Ellison's Enduring Impact

Title: Beyond the Horizon: Oracle's Future and Ellison's Timeless Legacy

As Larry Ellison's journey through the chapters of life, technology, and leadership reaches a pivotal moment, Chapter 6 unveils the lasting impact of his legacy and examines Oracle's future beyond his direct leadership. This chapter reflects on the broader implications of Ellison's influence on the tech industry, Oracle's position in the market, and the ongoing narrative of innovation and success.

The Evolution of Oracle: Sailing into the Future

Chapter 6 explores Oracle's trajectory as it sails into the future without Ellison at the helm. With a foundation built on decades of innovation and adaptability, Oracle's continued success hinges on its ability to navigate the ever-changing seas of technology. This section examines the strategies Oracle employs to maintain its relevance and leadership in a dynamic industry landscape.

Leadership Transition: Passing the Baton

As Ellison takes a step back from day-to-day operations, Chapter 6 delves into the dynamics of leadership transition within Oracle. The narrative explores how the company navigates the change in leadership, ensuring a smooth transition and continuity of the principles and values that have defined Oracle under Ellison's stewardship.

Emerging Technologies: New Horizons

The tech industry is ever-evolving, with new technologies constantly emerging on the horizon. Chapter 6 explores how Oracle, building on Ellison's legacy, continues to embrace innovation. From advancements in cloud computing to the integration of artificial intelligence, this section outlines how Oracle positions itself at the forefront of technological progress.

Philanthropy and Social Impact: A Continuing Voyage

Ellison's commitment to philanthropy is an enduring aspect of his legacy. Chapter 6 examines how Oracle, under new leadership, continues to contribute to social causes and global well-being. From educational initiatives to environmental sustainability, this section explores Oracle's ongoing efforts to make a positive impact beyond the realm of technology.

Reflections on Leadership: The Ripple Effect

Chapter 6 takes a retrospective look at the ripple effect of Ellison's leadership philosophy. From the corporate culture he cultivated to the impact on the broader tech industry, this section reflects on how Ellison's approach to leadership continues to influence not only Oracle but also serves as a source of inspiration for leaders across diverse sectors.

The Enduring Legacy: Beyond the Business

The final section of Chapter 6 reflects on Larry Ellison's enduring legacy. Beyond the business empire he built, Ellison's impact resonates in the realms of technology, philanthropy, and leadership. This chapter concludes by examining the timeless lessons that leaders and aspiring entrepreneurs can draw from Ellison's journey, creating a legacy that transcends individual success.

Join us as we unravel the final chapter of Larry Ellison's impactful narrative. Chapter 6 is a contemplation on legacy, transition, and the ever-expanding horizons that lie ahead for Oracle and the tech industry, echoing the enduring influence of a captain who boldly sailed through uncharted waters and left an indelible mark on the world.

7

Sailing Forward: Oracle's Continuing Odyssey in a Dynamic World

Title: Into the Next Chapter: Oracle's Ongoing Voyage of Innovation

As Oracle charts its course into the next chapter of its history, Chapter 7 delves into the company's continued odyssey in the ever-evolving landscape of technology. This chapter explores Oracle's ongoing commitment to innovation, its strategic initiatives, and the challenges and opportunities that lie ahead.

A Vision for the Future

Chapter 7 unfolds with a glimpse into Oracle's vision for the future. As the tech industry undergoes rapid transformations, Oracle sets its sights on new horizons. This section explores the company's strategic goals, including advancements in emerging technologies, industry partnerships, and its role in shaping the digital landscape.

Cloud Computing and Beyond

With cloud computing firmly established, Chapter 7 delves into how Oracle continues to leverage this technology to meet the evolving needs of businesses. The narrative explores Oracle's cloud strategy, innovations in cloud services, and the role of cloud computing in facilitating digital transformation for organizations across diverse industries.

Artificial Intelligence and Autonomous Systems

The chapter explores Oracle's endeavors in the realm of artificial intelligence and autonomous systems. As these technologies redefine the possibilities in data management, security, and business operations, Oracle's commitment to staying at the forefront of innovation is highlighted, showcasing the company's role in shaping the future of intelligent enterprise solutions.

Global Expansion and Market Dynamics

Oracle's global footprint continues to expand, and Chapter 7 explores the company's strategies for navigating diverse markets and adapting to regional dynamics. From addressing the unique needs of different industries to fostering international partnerships, this section unravels how Oracle remains a global leader with a keen understanding of the complexities of the international business landscape.

Corporate Social Responsibility in the 21st Century

As the importance of corporate social responsibility grows, Chapter 7 examines how Oracle continues to contribute to societal well-being. From initiatives addressing environmental sustainability to supporting education and community development, this section highlights Oracle's ongoing commitment to making a positive impact on a global scale.

Challenges on the Horizon

No journey is without challenges, and Chapter 7 acknowledges the obstacles that Oracle faces in an era marked by rapid technological advancements, geopolitical shifts, and evolving customer expectations. From cybersecurity concerns to market competition, this section explores how Oracle navigates the complexities of the digital age.

The Next Generation of Leadership

With a leadership transition underway, Chapter 7 sheds light on Oracle's approach to cultivating the next generation of leaders. The narrative explores the continuity of the company's core values and the importance of nurturing a culture of innovation, adaptability, and customer-centricity.

Sailing into Uncertain Seas

The final section of Chapter 7 reflects on the uncertainty that comes with sailing into the future. It explores Oracle's readiness to embrace change, tackle unforeseen challenges, and seize opportunities that may arise in the dynamic landscape of the tech industry.

Join us as we embark on the next chapter of Oracle's journey. Chapter 7 is a forward-looking exploration of the company's ongoing pursuit of innovation and its commitment to staying at the forefront of the technological tides, setting the stage for a new era in the ever-evolving world of business and technology.

8

Beyond Boundaries: Oracle's Impact on the Digital Frontier

Title: Trailblazing Beyond: Oracle's Influence on the Digital Landscape

As Oracle continues its journey into uncharted territories, Chapter 8 delves into the company's far-reaching impact on the digital frontier. This chapter explores Oracle's role in shaping the broader digital landscape, influencing industries, fostering innovation, and contributing to the ongoing evolution of the interconnected world.

Industries Transformed

Oracle's influence extends across diverse industries, and Chapter 8 begins by examining how the company has played a pivotal role in transforming sectors ranging from finance and healthcare to manufacturing and beyond. The narrative unfolds the stories of how Oracle's technological solutions have reshaped business operations, streamlined processes, and fostered unprecedented levels of efficiency.

The Intersection of Cloud, Big Data, and IoT

The convergence of cloud computing, big data analytics, and the Internet of Things (IoT) has ushered in a new era of possibilities. Chapter 8 explores Oracle's contributions at the intersection of these transformative technologies. From providing robust cloud infrastructure to enabling data-driven decision-making and leveraging IoT for smarter operations, Oracle's impact on the digital landscape is highlighted.

Global Connectivity and Collaboration

The digital landscape knows no borders, and Oracle has been at the forefront of fostering global connectivity and collaboration. Chapter 8 delves into the company's initiatives to create interconnected ecosystems, support cross-border collaborations, and facilitate the seamless flow of information in an increasingly interconnected world.

Ecosystem of Innovation: Oracle and Startups

Innovation often thrives in the dynamic space of startups, and Chapter 8 examines Oracle's role in nurturing the next generation of innovators. The narrative unfolds how Oracle's startup programs, investments, and partnerships contribute to the growth of entrepreneurial ecosystems and drive technological advancements.

Data Security and Privacy in the Digital Age

With the increasing digitization of information, data security and privacy have become paramount. Chapter 8 explores Oracle's commitment to safeguarding data in the digital age. From developing robust security solutions to advocating for responsible data management practices, Oracle's impact on establishing standards for data security is unraveled.

Future Trends and Technological Frontiers

The digital frontier is ever-expanding, and Chapter 8 explores Oracle's perspective on future trends and technological frontiers. From the role of artificial intelligence in shaping business strategies to the potential of quantum computing, this section provides insights into Oracle's vision for the next wave of technological advancements.

Corporate Citizenship: Oracle's Social Impact

Beyond business operations, Oracle's commitment to corporate citizenship is explored in Chapter 8. The narrative unfolds how the company contributes to social impact, environmental sustainability, and philanthropy, showcasing Oracle's dedication to making a positive difference in the communities it serves.

A Reflection on Oracle's Footprint

The chapter concludes with a reflection on Oracle's footprint on the digital landscape. From pioneering technologies to influencing global connectivity and advocating for ethical practices, Oracle's impact reverberates far beyond its own operations.

Join us as we explore the expansive influence of Oracle on the digital frontier. Chapter 8 is a testament to Oracle's enduring legacy as a trailblazer, shaping the course of the digital landscape and leaving an indelible mark on the interconnected world.

9

A Tapestry of Success: Larry Ellison's Enduring Legacy

Title: The Master Weaver: Larry Ellison's Legacy Woven in Time

As the chapters of Larry Ellison's life continue to unfold, Chapter 9 delves into the tapestry of success he has woven across the realms of technology, business, and philanthropy. This chapter reflects on the enduring legacy of a visionary leader and the threads of influence he has left in the fabric of the world.

The Architect of Innovation

Chapter 9 begins by examining Ellison's legacy as the architect of innovation. From the early days of Oracle to the forefront of emerging technologies, this section reflects on Ellison's role in shaping the technological landscape. His ability to envision the future, foster innovation, and lead Oracle through waves of change stands as a testament to his enduring impact.

Cultural Imprint: The Oracle Way

Ellison's leadership has not only shaped Oracle's trajectory but has also left an indelible mark on the company's culture. Chapter 9 explores the Oracle Way—the principles, values, and ethos that define the organization. From embracing risk to fostering a culture of continuous innovation, this section reflects on how Ellison's leadership philosophy has become ingrained in Oracle's DNA.

Shaping Industries, Empowering Businesses

The legacy of Ellison extends to the industries transformed by Oracle's technological solutions. Chapter 9 delves into how Oracle's products and services have empowered businesses, driving efficiency, innovation, and growth across various sectors. The narrative explores case studies and success stories that illuminate the tangible impact of Ellison's vision on the business landscape.

Philanthropy Beyond Measure

Beyond the boardroom, Ellison's legacy shines through his philanthropic endeavors. Chapter 9 reflects on the far-reaching impact of the Ellison Medical Foundation, educational initiatives, and contributions to societal well-being. The narrative explores how Ellison's commitment to philanthropy has created a lasting legacy of positive change.

Leadership Lessons for Tomorrow's Captains

The chapter unfolds with a focus on the leadership lessons embedded in Ellison's legacy. Aspiring leaders and entrepreneurs can draw inspiration from Ellison's journey—lessons of visionary thinking, calculated risk-taking, adaptability, and a commitment to making a positive impact. This section provides a roadmap for future captains navigating the seas of business and technology.

A Steward of the Environment

Ellison's legacy extends to his role as a steward of the environment. Chapter 9 explores his contributions to environmental sustainability, responsible land management on the island of Lanai, and Oracle's initiatives in reducing its ecological footprint. This section reflects on Ellison's commitment to balancing business success with environmental responsibility.

Reflections on the Personal Odyssey

As the narrative unfolds, Chapter 9 offers a reflective perspective on Ellison's personal odyssey. The highs, lows, triumphs, and challenges are woven into the fabric of a life lived with passion, determination, and a relentless pursuit of excellence. This section provides a glimpse into the personal reflections and sentiments that accompany a journey of such magnitude.

The Ever-Expanding Tapestry

The chapter concludes by acknowledging that Ellison's legacy is an ever-expanding tapestry, woven not only in the chapters of Oracle's history but in the broader narrative of technological progress, leadership excellence, and philanthropic impact. As Oracle sails into the future, Ellison's influence continues to ripple through time.

Join us as we unravel the final chapter of Larry Ellison's enduring legacy. Chapter 9 is a contemplation on the master weaver whose threads of innovation, leadership, and philanthropy have left an indelible mark on the canvas of the world—a legacy that continues to inspire, shape, and endure.

10

Sailing Into Tomorrow: Oracle's Future Horizons

Title: Beyond the Horizon: Oracle's Continued Odyssey

As we approach the conclusion of this narrative, Chapter 10 ventures into the future, exploring Oracle's ongoing journey into the unknown and the horizons that lie beyond. This chapter offers insights into Oracle's strategic directions, its role in the evolving tech landscape, and the company's commitment to innovation, continuity, and global impact.

Vision for Tomorrow

Chapter 10 begins by unveiling Oracle's vision for the future. With new leaders at the helm and a legacy of innovation behind, this section explores Oracle's strategic roadmap. From advancements in cloud services to pioneering technologies on the horizon, Oracle's vision sets the course for the company's continued relevance in a rapidly changing world.

The Next Wave of Technologies

As technology continues to advance, Oracle stands at the forefront of the next wave of innovations. Chapter 10 delves into emerging technologies that will shape Oracle's trajectory—from artificial intelligence and machine learning to quantum computing and beyond. The narrative unfolds Oracle's role in driving these technological frontiers and contributing to the digital transformation of industries.

Global Leadership and Industry Influence

Oracle's influence extends beyond its products and services; it shapes global conversations and industry dynamics. Chapter 10 reflects on Oracle's position as a thought leader, influencer, and contributor to industry standards. As the company navigates the challenges and opportunities in an interconnected world, this section explores Oracle's impact on shaping the digital narrative.

Expanding Ecosystems and Collaborations

Collaboration is key in the digital age, and Chapter 10 explores how Oracle continues to foster partnerships and expand its ecosystems. From collaborations with startups to industry alliances, this section delves into Oracle's approach to building networks that fuel innovation, enable global connectivity, and contribute to a collective digital future.

The Evolving Role of Data

Data remains a cornerstone of Oracle's business, and Chapter 10 reflects on the evolving role of data in the digital landscape. From data-driven decision-making to the ethical considerations surrounding data usage, this section explores Oracle's stance on responsible data practices and the company's contributions to shaping the future of data management.

Cultural Continuity and Innovation

The Oracle Way, ingrained in the company's culture, continues to guide Oracle into the future. Chapter 10 examines how cultural continuity, coupled with a commitment to innovation, forms the backbone of Oracle's resilience and adaptability. The narrative reflects on how the cultural fabric woven by Ellison persists in shaping Oracle's identity.

Nurturing Talent and Leadership

With the next generation of leaders emerging, Chapter 10 sheds light on Oracle's commitment to nurturing talent and leadership. From mentorship programs to initiatives that foster diversity and inclusion, this section explores how Oracle cultivates a dynamic and skilled workforce to navigate the complexities of the digital age.

Legacy of Responsibility: Corporate Citizenship

As Oracle sails into the future, the company's commitment to corporate citizenship remains steadfast. Chapter 10 reflects on Oracle's initiatives in environmental sustainability, philanthropy, and social responsibility. The narrative explores how Oracle's legacy of responsibility contributes to positive global impact.

The Journey Continues

The final section of Chapter 10 encapsulates the essence of Oracle's ongoing journey. As the company continues to sail into the future, the narrative reflects on the uncharted waters ahead, the challenges and triumphs that await, and the unwavering spirit that propels Oracle into tomorrow.

Join us as we embark on the final leg of Oracle's journey, navigating the uncharted waters of the future. Chapter 10 is a glimpse into the company's ongoing odyssey, a story yet to be fully written, and a testament to Oracle's commitment to charting the course of technological progress, innovation, and global impact.

11

Reflections and Resonance: Larry Ellison's Lasting Impact

Title: The Echoes of Success: Larry Ellison's Enduring Influence

As we conclude this narrative, Chapter 11 reflects on the profound and lasting impact of Larry Ellison—a visionary leader, innovator, and philanthropist. This chapter explores how Ellison's legacy resonates across the realms of technology, business, and philanthropy, leaving an indelible imprint on the world.

The Ripple Effect: Beyond Oracle's Horizon

Chapter 11 begins by exploring the ripple effect of Ellison's influence beyond Oracle's immediate horizon. The narrative reflects on the leaders, innovators, and entrepreneurs who have drawn inspiration from Ellison's journey, shaping their own paths and contributing to the ever-expanding tapestry of success in the tech industry.

Lessons from the Captain's Log

Ellison's life is a treasure trove of leadership lessons, and Chapter 11 distills these insights into a compendium of wisdom. From embracing innovation and calculated risk-taking to fostering a culture of continuous learning, the section provides actionable takeaways for leaders, business enthusiasts, and aspiring entrepreneurs.

Shaping the Narrative of Silicon Valley

As a pioneering figure in Silicon Valley, Ellison has played a crucial role in shaping the narrative of the tech industry. Chapter 11 reflects on how his journey has become intertwined with the larger story of Silicon Valley's evolution, contributing to the region's reputation as a global hub of innovation and technological advancement.

A Beacon for Future Innovators

Ellison's legacy serves as a beacon for future innovators and leaders. This section explores how his fearless pursuit of ambitious goals, coupled with a commitment to technological excellence, continues to inspire a new generation of trailblazers who dare to dream beyond boundaries.

Philanthropy's Enduring Impact

The chapter unfolds with an exploration of how Ellison's philanthropic endeavors endure, creating a lasting impact on medical research, education, environmental conservation, and societal well-being. From the Ellison Medical Foundation to educational initiatives, this section reflects on the ongoing contributions to making a positive difference in the world.

A Life Well Lived

As we reflect on the entirety of Larry Ellison's journey, Chapter 11 acknowledges the completeness of a life well lived—a life marked by triumphs, challenges, innovation, and philanthropy. The narrative encapsulates the essence of Ellison's legacy as a multifaceted tapestry woven with the threads of success, compassion, and a relentless pursuit of excellence.

The Echoes Continue

The echoes of Larry Ellison's influence reverberate far beyond the confines of this narrative. As Chapter 11 concludes, it recognizes that the echoes continue—through Oracle's ongoing journey, in the lessons imparted, and in the profound impact made on the digital landscape and beyond.

Join us as we bid farewell to the pages of this narrative, acknowledging the enduring resonance of Larry Ellison's legacy. Chapter 11 is a reflection on a life that has left an indelible mark on the world—a mark that continues to echo through time, inspiring and shaping the narratives yet to unfold.

12

The Unfinished Symphony: Oracle's Future Symphony

Title: The Ongoing Overture: Oracle's Unfinished Symphony

As we turn the page to Chapter 12, we find ourselves at the precipice of the future—an unwritten chapter in Oracle's enduring saga. This concluding chapter explores the anticipation, possibilities, and the symphony yet to be composed as Oracle continues its journey into the uncharted realms of technology, business, and innovation.

Prelude to Innovation

Chapter 12 opens with a prelude to the future—an exploration of the innovation landscape that Oracle is poised to traverse. From cutting-edge technologies to emerging trends, this section sets the stage for the next wave of advancements that will shape Oracle's ongoing narrative.

The Symphony of Emerging Technologies

As technology continues its relentless march forward, the narrative unfolds the symphony of emerging technologies that Oracle will navigate. From artificial intelligence and blockchain to quantum computing and beyond, this section explores how Oracle plans to harmonize these elements into its orchestration of products and services.

Orchestrating Industry Solutions

The chapter delves into Oracle's role as an orchestrator of industry solutions. As businesses evolve, so too must the symphony of tools and services that Oracle provides. This section reflects on how Oracle will compose solutions that resonate with the diverse needs of industries, ensuring relevance and impact in an ever-changing landscape.

Global Harmony: Oracle in the International Arena

Oracle's global presence and influence come to the forefront in this section. As the company conducts its symphony on the international stage, the narrative explores how Oracle will harmonize with the unique dynamics, challenges, and opportunities presented by different regions and markets.

Sustainably Composed: Oracle's Environmental Allegro

Environmental sustainability takes center stage in this movement. Chapter 12 reflects on how Oracle, as a responsible corporate citizen, will compose its environmental allegro—contributing to a harmonious balance between business success and ecological stewardship.

Data, Security, and the Sonata of Ethical Practices

The symphony of data plays a pivotal role in Oracle's future composition. This section explores how Oracle will continue to conduct the sonata of ethical data practices and security measures, ensuring a harmonious relationship with its customers and stakeholders.

The Conductor's Baton: Leadership in Transition

With a leadership transition underway, the chapter reflects on the conductor's baton passing to new hands. As Oracle welcomes a new era of leadership, the narrative explores the continuity of the Oracle Way and how the new leaders will wield the baton to guide the symphony into the future.

Coda of Continuity: Embracing the Unfinished

As Chapter 12 draws to a close, the narrative explores the coda of continuity—a reflection on Oracle's commitment to embracing the unfinished. This section acknowledges that the symphony is an ongoing composition, with each note building on the melodies of the past and paving the way for future crescendos.

The Uncharted Crescendo

The chapter concludes with an anticipation of the uncharted crescendo—the unwritten symphony that Oracle is yet to compose. As the company sails into unexplored waters, the narrative leaves room for the crescendo of innovation, success, and positive impact that will resonate through Oracle's ongoing journey.

Join us as we conclude this narrative, standing on the threshold of Oracle's future symphony. Chapter 12 is a prelude to the unwritten melodies, an exploration of the possibilities yet to be realized, and an acknowledgment that Oracle's symphony is an ever-evolving composition—one that continues to captivate and inspire the world.

13

Summary

"Sailing to Success: Larry Ellison's Life Lessons from America's Cup to Oracle's Helm" is a comprehensive exploration of the life, career, and impact of Larry Ellison, the co-founder of Oracle Corporation. The narrative spans 12 chapters, each focusing on different aspects of Ellison's journey and Oracle's evolution. Here's a summary:

1. Chapter 1: Setting Sail
   - Introduces Larry Ellison's early life and passion for sailing.
   - Explores the parallels between sailing and Ellison's approach to business.
   - Highlights the competitive spirit that drove him to success.

2. Chapter 2: Navigating the Tech Seas
   - Details Ellison's entry into the tech industry.
   - Explores Oracle's early days and the development of the relational database.
   - Highlights Ellison's strategic thinking and competitive edge.

3. Chapter 3: Sailing the Digital Seas
   - Explores Oracle's transition to cloud computing and AI under Ellison's leadership.
   - Discusses key acquisitions and the company's focus on security.

SUMMARY

   - Examines Oracle's initiatives in corporate social responsibility and sustainability.

4. Chapter 4: Beyond Business
   - Delves into Ellison's philanthropic efforts.
   - Explores initiatives in medical research, education, and environmental conservation.
   - Highlights Ellison's multifaceted impact beyond the business realm.

5. Chapter 5: Mastering the Waves of Change
   - Explores Ellison's leadership philosophy.
   - Discusses visionary leadership, risk-taking, and innovation.
   - Examines Oracle's adaptability in the face of industry challenges.

6. Chapter 6: Legacy Unveiled
   - Reflects on Oracle's trajectory as Ellison steps back from day-to-day operations.
   - Examines the leadership transition and ongoing impact.
   - Explores Oracle's commitment to innovation and corporate social responsibility.

7. Chapter 7: Sailing Forward
   - Explores Oracle's future direction and vision.
   - Discusses advancements in cloud computing, AI, and global expansion.
   - Examines Oracle's role in the digital transformation of industries.

8. Chapter 8: Beyond Boundaries
   - Explores Oracle's impact on the broader digital landscape.
   - Discusses global connectivity, collaborations, and Oracle's role in innovation ecosystems.
   - Examines Oracle's initiatives in data security, privacy, and corporate citizenship.

9. Chapter 9: A Tapestry of Success
   - Reflects on Ellison's legacy as an innovator and leader.
   - Explores the cultural imprint of the Oracle Way.
   - Discusses the impact of Oracle's products and services on various industries.

10. Chapter 10: Sailing Into Tomorrow
    - Explores Oracle's vision for the future.
    - Discusses the next wave of technologies, global leadership, and industry influence.
    - Examines Oracle's role in nurturing talent, leadership, and corporate citizenship.

11. Chapter 11: Reflections and Resonance
    - Reflects on the lasting impact of Larry Ellison.
    - Explores lessons from Ellison's leadership and philanthropy.
    - Discusses how Ellison has shaped the narrative of Silicon Valley.

12. Chapter 12: The Unfinished Symphony
    - Explores Oracle's future direction and ongoing journey.
    - Discusses the symphony of emerging technologies, industry solutions, and global harmony.
    - Reflects on leadership in transition and Oracle's commitment to an unfinished but harmonious future.

Throughout the narrative, the story unfolds as a dynamic interplay of personal and professional elements, showcasing Larry Ellison's prowess as a leader, innovator, and philanthropist, while also providing insights into Oracle's evolving role in the ever-changing landscape of technology.

www.ingramcontent.com/pod-product-compliance
Lightning Source LLC
LaVergne TN
LVHW010438070526
838199LV00066B/6077